FIND YOUR TALENT

MAKE A PODCAST!

Matt Anniss

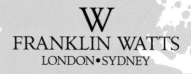

FRANKLIN WATTS
LONDON • SYDNEY

This paperback edition published in 2014

First published in 2012 by Franklin Watts

Copyright © 2012 Arcturus Publishing Limited

Franklin Watts
338 Euston Road
London NW1 3BH

Franklin Watts Australia
Level 17/207 Kent Street, Sydney NSW 2000

Produced by Arcturus Publishing Limited,
26/27 Bickels Yard, 151–153 Bermondsey Street, London SE1 3HA

Text: Matt Anniss
Editors: Joe Harris and Sarah Eason
Design: Paul Myerscough
Cover design: Akihiro Nakayama

Picture credits:
Cover images: iStockphoto: Yurovskikh Aleksander cr, Rapid Eye Media br; Shutterstock: Creatista ccr, Mike Flippo tr, Goodluz bl, Kzenon tl, nikkytok ccl, Dmitriy Shironosov ct, Jason Stitt bc, Tsian tc, Tonis Valing cl.
Interior images: Bebo: 22bl; Dreamstime: Nikhil Gangavane 19b, Dennis Owusu-ansah 18bl, Alexandr Stepanov 4tr; Szefei 14bl, Arman Zhenikeyev 15br; Shutterstock: 2happy 7b, Yuri Arcurs 16b, Basel101658 27tr, Doctor Bass 15bl, Domen Colja 10bc, Distinctive Images 3cl, 8tr, Vereshchagin Dmitry 25cl, Jaimie Duplass 6bl, Erikona 26tr, Harmony Gerber 5tr, Goodluz 29br, Andreas Gradin 23tr, Mark Hryciw 6tr, Iconspro 17tl, Monkey Business Images 13tc, 28br, Florian Ispas 25tl, Jeka 21br, Karin Hildebrand Lau 22br, Lori Martin 18tr, Netfalls 10bl, Qingqing 5bl, Roca 9tr, Yuri Shchipakin 20–21, Dmitriy Shironosov 01, Sianc 11br, Vitaly Titov/Maria Sidelnikova 8bl, Thelefty 24–25c, Devation/Edwin Verbruggen 17cl, OtnaYdur 3bl, 12–13bc; Brandon Tucker: 26br.

A CIP catalogue record for this book is available from the British Library.

Dewey Decimal Classification Number 006.7'876-dc23

ISBN-13: 978 1 4451 3127 6

Printed in China

Franklin Watts is a division of Hachette Children's Books, an Hachette UK company.
www.hachette.co.uk

SL002138EN
Supplier 03 Date 1113 Print run 3062

CONTENTS

FIND YOUR TALENT!

Not only is it a fun hobby, but creating your own podcast could lead to a successful career in radio.

Have you ever dreamed about being a radio star? Would you like to create something that thousands of people listen to every week? Maybe you would love to make people laugh, share your ideas or showcase new music? If the answer to any of these questions is yes, you could be the next big podcast star!

Podcast dreams Every day, hundreds of thousands of people around the world record new 'podcasts'. These are short audio shows that can be listened to on computers, mobile phones and portable music devices. Anyone can make a podcast – all you need is a computer, a microphone and lots of ideas.

Going global If you've got a good idea, you can turn it into a podcast. In time, that podcast could lead to bigger and better things. Since people started making podcasts in 2004, many 'podcasters' have gone on to have great careers as radio DJs, journalists and comedians. Some podcasters have even been given their own TV shows, while others have set new world records and won awards.

RICKY GERVAIS

INSIDE STORY:

In 2006, well-known comedian and actor Ricky Gervais teamed up with The Guardian newspaper to launch his weekly podcast. The podcast was an amazing success, and was downloaded more than 270,000 times a week! In 2007, it was named the world's most popular podcast by The Guinness Book of World Records. Gervais says 'The podcast is the thing I have most fun with – more than Extras, The Office or The Simpsons.'

The podcast series created by Ricky Gervais, Stephen Merchant and Karl Pilkington was so popular that it was turned into an animated TV series.

Podcasts are popular partly because they can be listened to on all sorts of devices, including MP3 players, computers and mobile phones.

Let's go! In this book, you'll find out that making your own podcast is quick, easy and lots of fun. You'll also discover a few real-life success stories behind some of the world's most popular podcasts, and find out how podcasters have turned their hobby into a fantastic career.

THE PODCAST STORY

Before you can start thinking about making your own podcast, let's find out how podcasts work and why they're so popular.

Audio and video Podcasts are short radio shows or, in the case of video podcasts, TV shows. They are usually made without high-tech studios or any training. Podcasts can vary in length from five minutes to several hours. They can be played on computers and mobile devices such as MP3 players and smartphones.

Richard Vobes became an internet sensation thanks to his comedy podcast, which features weird stunts like this one.

Podcasts don't have to be talk-based. Some of the most popular podcasts feature DJ mixes or musical selections.

Podcast great

EARLY DAYS:

Part-time British comedian Richard Vobes is the man behind one of the longest-running podcasts to date, *The Vobes Radio Show*. He started his show in a beach hut in Worthing, UK, in 2005. Today, he has recorded over 1,000 episodes of his five-times-a-week podcast. His brand of madcap comedy proved so popular that listeners donated money to send him on a road trip to the USA! While there, he recorded a week's worth of shows.

GO FOR IT: LISTEN IN

To listen to a podcast, try the following:

- Open up the iTunes programme (if you have it on your computer) and click on the tab marked 'podcasts', or search for 'podcast directory' on Google.
- Look through the lists of podcasts and click on links to download any that interest you.
- Listen to the podcast on your computer or mobile device.

One-offs or episodes? Podcasts can be one-off shows, but most are created as a series of episodes. They can be broadcast daily, weekly, fortnightly or monthly. Listeners can subscribe to shows through services such as the iTunes Podcast Directory or PodOmatic.

Anything goes Podcasts can be about anything, from popular topics such as sport, movies, news and politics to more specialist subjects such as hobbies, business and computing. They can feature comedy sketches or short radio plays, music mixes or topical debates. When it comes to podcasting, the choice is yours!

Podcasts can be about anything you like, from popular hobbies to extreme sports such as skydiving.

WHAT'S YOUR BIG IDEA?

The most successful podcasts offer something special. Some feature topics people want to know more about or that lots of people are interested in. Others set out simply to entertain their listeners. So, what will you choose?

Information on tap Some of the most popular podcasts focus on a particular subject and offer advice. Some review films, books, restaurants or tourist attractions. Others serve up recipes, help people to learn a language or give advice about a particular subject, such as computers.

Many successful podcasts focus on issues that touch people's lives, such as religion or current affairs.

Your podcast doesn't have to be serious – many of the most popular podcasts feature comedy sketches, humorous stories or funny situations.

TEENAGE DREAMS

INSIDE STORY:

Californian music fan Martina Butler created the Emo Girl Talk podcast and website in 2005. She was just 15 years old at the time. Martina's mix of music, advice and chat soon had a large following. 'I was the first teenage podcaster to receive corporate sponsorship to fund the site,' Martina told The New York Times in 2008. 'It's only getting bigger for me!' Inspired by her success, Martina now has her sights set on a TV career.

Get creative Some of the most successful podcasts are designed to make people laugh, while others feature a new dramatic episode every week. Some podcasters create their own weekly soap opera, or read out their short stories.

If your passion is for an exciting sport such as BMX biking, you could use your podcast to offer news, advice and features of interest to other enthusiasts.

Choosing your content
Whatever you decide to do, remember that 'content is king'. Content is the mix of information you have on your podcast, from interviews to news reports. If you have great content that will appeal to listeners, your podcast has a greater chance of success.

GO FOR IT: WHAT'S SO SPECIAL?

Try the following to work out what's special about your podcast:

- Listen to some popular podcasts as research to see what works and what doesn't. Discover the themes and subjects that are not already covered.
- Jot down a list of possible themes for your podcast.
- Note any topics that you might want to cover.
- Write down a list of names for your podcast.

GET THE GEAR

If you're going to dive head-first into the exciting world of podcasting, you'll need to make sure you've got all the equipment you need. Luckily, you don't need a lot to get started.

Podcasting didn't start until 2004. However, web developers were experimenting with short sound recordings in the late 1990s. These podcast-like recordings were just quick interviews with other computer users. They were then offered as MP3 downloads on websites. Website users could 'subscribe' to these sound recordings and then listen to them. Within a few years, the idea had caught on. People began to create short, talk-only 'podcasts' for their friends' MP3 players.

Head to hardware The three most important things you'll need to create your first podcast are a computer (either a PC or a Mac), a microphone and a pair of headphones. You'll need the computer to record and edit your podcast and the microphone to record your voiceovers. You'll use the headphones to check sound levels and listen back to recordings. If you've not got access to equipment at home, your school or library may have equipment you can use or borrow.

It's possible to record a podcast without a separate microphone, but you may find that the sound quality is not good.

Software solutions Once you have your computer, microphone and headphones in place, you'll need some software that allows you to record and edit your work, and arrange voice and music recordings to create a podcast. The most widely-used free recording software program is Audacity, which is available for both PC and Mac.

Simple set-up Once you've downloaded and installed some recording software onto your computer, you'll then need to plug the microphone and headphones in, too. Then you are ready to start!

Before recording your podcast, it's a good idea to practise recording yourself speaking into the microphone:

- Open up your recording software programme.
- Press record and speak a few sentences into the microphone.
- Stop the recording when you've finished, and press play to listen back.

It's important to listen back to your recordings. By doing so you can check the recordings, judge their quality and evaluate your own mic technique.

PERFECT PLANNING

I f you want your podcast to attract and impress listeners, it must sound professional. It should also offer a good mix of subjects, themes and segments. It is best to plan your content before you put your podcast together.

Time limits Podcasts can vary in length, but most are between 30 minutes and an hour long. This is a lot of time to fill for a beginner! It's best to make your first podcast much shorter – aim for about five to ten minutes.

Recording a podcast can be a lengthy process. Many podcasters work on their episodes with groups of friends. It cuts down the work – and makes it more fun!

INSIDE STORY: FILMSPOTTING

Movie fan Adam Kempenaar is one of the men behind Filmspotting. This popular weekly film review podcast has been running since 2005. Adam believes that the success of his podcast is down to its format. 'We always make sure that the show has a clear structure with segments people could look forward to each week, such as the Top Five,' he told the Atomic Podcasts blog in 2009. 'I'd definitely encourage aspiring podcasters to develop a format for their show.'

The more the merrier

Now is as good a time as any to decide whether you're going to put together your podcast alone, or share the workload with a partner or group of friends. Many successful podcasts are written and presented by two or more people. Working with other people can be a lot of fun. It also allows you to talk about different ideas and divide up the work.

Some podcasters find it useful to write a script for their recordings beforehand, so that they sound more professional.

GO FOR IT: SCRIPT WORK

Not all podcasters work from scripts. Some prefer to work from rough lists of discussion topics or themes. However, for first-time podcasters, putting together a script can be a great way to get started:

- Write down exactly what you want to say in your podcast. Start by telling listeners who you are and what the podcast is about. At the end, you could thank people for listening and ask them to tune in next week.
- When you're happy with the script, read it aloud and time yourself to see how long it is.
- If the script is too short or too long, re-write it until it's roughly the right length.

Killer content The next task is to decide what you're going to talk about in your first podcast, and for how long. Will you just share your thoughts on a particular subject? Are you also going to include interviews with other people, music clips or panel discussions, perhaps with your friends? Many podcasts include regular features such as a 'tip of the week' or a review section.

START RECORDING

You've got the gear and installed your recording software. You've brainstormed ideas, locked down your format and written a watertight script. Now, it's time to put all of that into practice and record your first-ever podcast!

Getting ready Before you set about recording your podcast, it's a good idea to get to know your script really well. Read it out loud a few times to get used to saying the words in a natural way. The best podcasters have a chatty microphone style, as if they're talking directly to the listener.

GO FOR IT: AND RECORD

When you're ready to record, just go for it:

- Go through your script, remembering to sound friendly and not too formal. Imagine you are talking directly to the listener, or a friend. This is your podcast, so let your personality shine through!
- If you make mistakes, just pause and say your lines again. Any errors can be removed in the editing process.
- When you've finished, stop the recording and listen to it. How does it sound?

Practise reading out your script before you record it. This allows you to perfect your presentation style before recording.

Helping hands By now, you may have decided to get some friends involved in your podcast. If not, it could still be useful to ask someone to lend a hand with your first recording. You could invite a friend to help, or ask an adult to work the recording software so you can concentrate on getting your voiceover right.

Watch the wave As you record, you'll see a waveform appear on your computer screen. It is important to check these sound waves – if the sound levels are too high (below), the wave will be very big and tall. This is a sign that your recording may become distorted.

Before recording your podcast, do a quick microphone test to check the sounds levels are okay. And make sure your equipment is correctly plugged in!

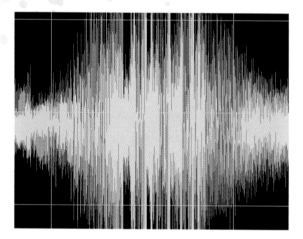

Listen out If the sound levels are too low (below), the wave will be narrow and short. This means that listeners may find it hard to hear what you are saying! Test your equipment to try to get the sound levels just right.

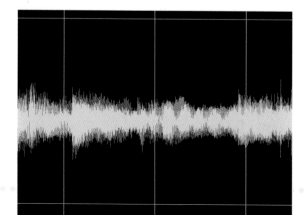

CREDIT TO THE EDIT

By editing your recording, you can transform it from a simple voice recording into a polished podcast production. It can be tricky at first, but with a little practice, you'll soon be editing like a pro!

Cut and paste

Software such as Audacity makes editing much easier. Your recording will appear on screen as a waveform. You can then use your computer mouse or laptop trackpad to highlight sections of the recording, then copy or cut them using specific tools. It might seem tricky at first, but it's actually very easy to do. To start, follow your editing program's tutorial.

Editing can be a daunting process at first, so don't be scared to ask for help if you think you need it.

Razor sharp The key to good editing is to make sure listeners can't hear your edits. The best way to do this when editing speech recordings is to cut entire questions or sentences. Another great trick is to use your editing software's zoom function to magnify the waveform on screen. By doing this, you can often spot exactly where a person beings to speak, and where they end.

Just the right size Once you are used to editing, you should be able to cut your podcast down to size. Remember, you have a ten-minute time limit for your first podcast, so cut it to fit. Don't worry if you do not get all the edits right at first. Just keep saving your recording as you work on it. If you make a mistake, you can then go back to the saved version.

Using the zoom function of your editing software will allow you to see the waveform up close and work out exactly where to cut to achieve the best edit.

Using jingles and musical 'stings' can liven up your podcast and make it sound more professional.

Layer it up Audio editing software can help you to be really creative, too. You can add music, sound effects and even radio-style jingles. Get together with your friends if they have instruments and play music. You could even record a short signature tune for your podcast. Take a look at the Audacity website (see page 31) for ideas.

GO FOR IT: MAKE AN MP3 FILE

To share your podcast with the world, you'll need to save or export it as an MP3 file. This is easy to do:
- Go to the Audacity website and look for the tutorial about exporting MP3s.
- Follow the instructions.
- Once you've exported your podcast as an MP3, listen to it in iTunes or Windows Media Player.

FROM SHOW TO SERIES

By now, you should happily be listening to an MP3 file of your first-ever podcast! Congratulations – this is a fantastic achievement. Now let's look at what you need to do to turn your podcast into a long-lasting success.

Series link The world's most popular podcasts are all episodic. This means they appear as individual episodes. The success of any podcast is judged on how many subscribers it has – people who choose to regularly listen to a podcast. A great way to gain dedicated listeners is to make sure you regularly broadcast new episodes.

Ministry of Slam has become one of the world's most popular wrestling podcasts.

The success of a podcast is often judged by how many subscribers it has.

MINISTRY OF SLAM

INSIDE STORY:

Weekly professional wrestling show Ministry of Slam has built up a huge fan base over recent years. Much of its success is down to its regular 'expert' features. Martin Mathers, Ministry of Slam's 'expert insider' says: 'Regular slots can help make planning your shows easier, give some consistency to the podcast and give listeners something to look forward to.'

Mix it up One key to a successful long-running podcast series is to keep material fresh. It's for this reason that many podcasts are set up in a similar way to a radio show. They have regular segments that feature the latest news, and discussions and interviews to keep up an audience's interest.

Find your voice Another important part of the podcast process is to find your own 'voice' and style. Podcasts that stand out from the crowd don't copy other people, but offer something new. In the case of your podcast, this could be your hosting style or a special mix of content. Whatever it is, offering something special is the key to podcasting success.

Featuring interviews with interesting people or celebrities can help to keep your podcasts fresh for regular listeners.

GOING LIVE

The next stage in your podcast journey is to share it with the world. This means getting it online and listed in the internet's biggest podcast directories.

Share the show Podcast directories are websites that list thousands of podcasts. They allow podcasters to share their shows with an army of potential listeners. See page 31 to find some popular podcast directories.

GO FOR IT: NAME THAT PODCAST

Before finding a podcast host, you need to put together a little bit of information about your podcast to interest would-be listeners. Try this:
- Decide on a name for your podcast. Ideally, the name should be short, snappy, memorable and self-explanatory. For example, if your podcast is about Canadian wildlife, you could call it 'Wild about Canada'. If it's about amateur astronomy, you could call it 'Starcast'.
- Write a short description of your first episode and the aims of your podcast series.

The host with the most Some podcast directories also offer to 'host' your podcasts. This means that they'll permanently store your shows on their servers. Most hosts will also take care of all the complicated work for you, such as creating a permanent website address and an RSS feed (see page 30). They'll also give you space to tell would-be listeners a little bit more about your podcast.

GO FOR IT: GET ON ITUNES

iTunes doesn't host podcasts, but it lists them. To get your podcast listed on iTunes:
- Go to the following website and read the detailed instructions: www.apple.com/itunes/podcasts/specs.html.
- Follow the directions to submit your podcast to iTunes.
- If your podcast is accepted (most are), you will receive a confirmation email.

When choosing a name, think about the content of your podcast, your own personality and the image you want to get across.

Upload time If you're ready to get your podcast online, you'll need to choose a host. Sites such as PodOmatic and Podcast Alley will store your podcasts for free. Other services such as Libsyn will do this for a small annual fee.

Take your time when choosing a host for your episodes – it's one of the biggest decisions you'll have to make about your podcast.

SPREAD THE WORD!

If your podcast is going to pick up a worldwide following, you'll need to let the world know about it. There are lots of ways you can do this.

Shout about it! The easiest way to let people know about your new podcast is to post messages on social networks and internet forums. Many successful podcasters set up pages and groups on sites such as Facebook and Bebo. Others set up a Twitter account to 'tweet' about new episodes and features.

Social networking sites such as Bebo and Facebook can be used to build up a fan base for your podcast series.

Feel the forum force! Internet forums are great for marketing because they allow you to easily target people who are interested in your subject or topic.

Get involved A great way to keep listeners is to make them feel part of the show. Many successful podcasters ask their listeners to send in questions, comments and suggestions. They can do this by email or Twitter. The messages are read out on the show and any questions answered.

Many successful podcasters use Twitter and SMS text messages to tell friends and potential listeners about their episodes.

GO FOR IT: TELL EVERYONE

Posting information about your podcast on an internet forum or message board is easy and free:

- Search the internet for forums and message boards that concentrate on the subject of your podcast.
- Sign-up for an account.
- Post a new message telling other forum users about your podcast.

If your podcast is about a popular topic such as street dance, you can use specialist forums and message boards to reach thousands of potential listeners.

INSIDE STORY: BEST OF YOUTUBE

The Best of YouTube is a weekly video podcast that has taken the world by storm. It allows viewers to submit and vote on its content. 'Most of the videos we feature are submitted to us by members of the public through our website, www.bestofyoutube. com,' podcast founder Lars Thorn explains. 'If successful, it will be posted to the website so users can vote on it. The top-rated videos are then featured in the weekly podcast.'

GUEST STARS

Special guests and interviews are one of the biggest pulls of many top podcasts. This is because they often give a fresh viewpoint that grabs the interest of both new and regular listeners.

Expert opinion Whatever the subject of your podcast, there are bound to be people that you could interview. Interviews help to hook the interest of your listeners. Everyone has a story, whether they're an expert in karate, a local politician or a musician or sports star. And if your star guest enjoys talking to you, they might even become a regular 'special guest' who will answer listeners' questions.

GO FOR IT: YOUR FIRST INTERVIEW

The most successful and popular podcasts can secure interviews with global stars such as Usain Bolt.

Here's how to carry out a successful interview:
- Find someone you'd like to interview – perhaps a friend who has something interesting to discuss, such as a fun hobby.
- Ask the person to come for an interview. Before you interview them, write down a list of questions you'd like to ask.
- When recording the interview, remember to listen to what they say instead of just thinking about your next question. The responses might make you think of a new question or suggest a topic to discuss.

When looking for places to carry out interviews with guest stars, try looking for quiet rooms with low ceilings. These often produce the best recordings.

INSIDE STORY:

BASEBALL PROSPECTUS RADIO

Baseball Prospectus Radio podcast host Will Carroll has made a name for himself by interviewing a wide range of sports people including club owners, fans and journalists. 'Players seldom give the most interesting interviews,' Will told the *Atomic Podcasts* blog. 'By going to that next tier – the guys that help make decisions or have an interesting viewpoint – we're giving a different insight into the game.'

Using a portable recording device like this one will allow you to record interviews with guest stars wherever you are.

Interviews on the go

Most interviews happen at a place that suits the guest. That means you might not be able to record them directly onto your computer. You may have to record them on another device and then transfer the recording to your computer so that you can edit it later. Most mobile phones, especially smartphones, feature voice recorders for recording interviews 'on the go'.

VODCAST DREAMS

Today, video podcasts, or 'vodcasts', are incredibly popular on sites such as YouTube and Vimeo. If you decide to switch to video, it could take your podcast to the next level!

Funny videos of animals make great clips for vodcasts and often prove to be hugely popular on video sharing sites such as YouTube.

Video killed the radio star If regular podcasts offer a chance to make your own short radio show, video podcasts allow you to put together short TV shows. Because of this, video podcasting is very popular with young comedians, would-be TV stars and anyone whose practical advice relies on showing images. Video podcasts are harder to make than regular podcasts, but the good news is you can be far more creative with them.

Star story Many video podcasters have been spotted by TV companies and offered their own 'pilots', or new shows on network websites. If you have a great idea for a short, entertaining TV show, video podcasting could be for you.

INSIDE STORY: SCAM SCHOOL

Magician Brian Brushwood had an unusual path to fame – he became a star through his *Scam School* video podcast. Brian uses it not only to showcase his bizarre brand of magic, but also to explain the methods behind popular tricks. 'After my first TV deal tanked, I was pretty ticked,' he explained in 2009. 'That's when I got interested in podcasts. It was an opportunity for someone like me without a big, established name to have much more creative control over my shows.'

Magician Brian Brushwood turned his fortunes around by creating his own video podcasts. These proved hugely successful on YouTube and turned him into a star.

Do-it-yourself You don't necessarily need a lot of equipment to make your own video podcasts. You could film segments or interviews on your mobile phone or digital camera, or borrow a video camera from your school or a friend.

Slice and dice To complete your 'vodcast', you'll need some video editing software. Most new PCs have Windows Movie Maker, while Macs feature iMovie. There are also plenty of free video editing packages available (see page 31 for suggestions). Once you have filmed and edited your video podcast, you can add it to the YouTube website for free.

If you like the idea of creating your own video podcasts, why not borrow some equipment and give it a go?

STEP UP A GEAR

By now, you may be an enthusiastic podcaster. You may have a string of shows to your name and a rising online profile. If so, it's time to think about how you can become a master podcaster!

Create jingles   Radio-style jingles can add interest to your podcast. They can be used at the beginning and end of shows, and even between segments. Don't worry if you have not used jingles before. Software programs such as Audacity include plenty of tools and features to help you on your way.

Tag on a tagline   Many successful podcasts have their own tagline. This is a slogan that's used both in the show and to market a podcast online. Like jingles, a catchy, relevant or funny slogan will help listeners to identify your show. If your show has a title that doesn't obviously suggest the subject you're discussing, then a slogan is essential.

Make a website   Having your own website can help people to find your podcast more easily. It can also give you a chance to upload extra material, such as longer versions of features, special episodes or video interviews. You can also add a forum for regular listeners and give would-be fans more information about your activities.

Fine-tune your shows   However good your podcasts are, there's always room for improvement. You should regularly review your episodes to see what works and what doesn't. If you got great responses to an episode about your skiing trip, include another one – people will want to hear more.

Use music Even talk-heavy podcasts benefit from a little music. If your topics are serious, a touch of music played in the background can liven things up. Music can be added in Audacity – check their website for details.

Making your podcast a success takes more than just great episodes. If you want to attract listeners and subscribers, you'll have to work hard at both content and marketing.

Taking criticism Although your podcast is your pet project, try to take criticism well. Some will be constructive and help you to improve your podcast. However, don't let negative comments discourage you. Some people may be critical no matter how good your podcast is. Even the best podcasters sometimes get one-star reviews on iTunes.

GLOSSARY

annual fee a charge for a service that is payable once a year

aspiring wanting to become something

audio recorded sound

awards prizes

brainstormed thought about intensely

broadcast distributing video or audio material

comedy sketches short, funny segments

consistency keeping something the same or similar

corporate sponsorship financial support given by a company or corporation

debates heated discussions

dedicated to be committed to something

device a mechanical tool, such as a mobile phone or digital recorder

directories detailed lists of something, for example phone numbers or podcasts

donated given free of charge

edit the process of changing, shortening or lengthening text, sound or video

episodes individual programmes or podcasts that fit into a continuing series

established well known

export to change a computer file into another form, or to send it somewhere

format a style used throughout a podcast or series of podcasts

forums website sections on which people discuss subjects that interest them

host a company specialising in the storage of websites, podcasts or blogs

hosting style your own particular way of presenting a podcast

insight a detailed view about a subject

installed stored on a computer

jingles short, catchy and memorable bursts of music and speech

journalists people who write or speak about subjects such as the news

magnify to make bigger

marketing making people aware of a product or service

microphone test checking that a microphone is working before recording

music clips short bursts of recorded music

network websites websites of big TV or radio 'networks' such as the BBC in the UK and NBC in the USA

online any activity on the internet

panel discussions a number of people talking with each other about a particular subject

portable music devices gadgets used to store and play music, for example iPods

review to give your opinion about something

review section a segment of a podcast devoted entirely to reviews

RSS feed the automated service that tells your fans when you upload a new episode to your podcast

segments short sections of a podcast or show devoted to different topics

servers huge banks of computers used to store large amounts of information

showcase to display or 'show off' something

slogan a memorable sentence or phrase

sound levels the volume of sound

submit to give something

subscribe to pay money to receive something regularly

tier a level

topics interesting subjects such as sport or the news

trackpad the part of a laptop that functions in the same way as a computer mouse

transfer to move something to another place

tutorial a lesson

voiceovers when a person speaks on a radio or TV recording, but is not seen

zoom function a tool that allows you to make something much bigger

FURTHER INFORMATION

Books

Podcasting for Dummies by Tee Morris, Chuck Tomasi and Evo Terra (John Wiley & Sons, 2008)

Podcast Solutions: The Complete Guide to Audio and Video Podcasting by Michael Geoghegan and Dan Klass (Friends of ED, 2007)

Podcasting: The Do-It-Yourself Guide by Todd Cochrane (John Wiley & Sons, 2005)

Websites

Audacity
Check out this popular free audio editing software package for PC and Mac:
www. audacity.sourceforge.net

Emo Girl Talk
Take a look at the popular, long-running American podcast run by college student Martina Butler:
www.americanheartbreak.com/emogirlwp

How to Podcast
Visit this excellent beginner's guide to the world of podcasting:
www.how-to-podcast-tutorial.com

iTunes
Apple's free media player software for Mac and PC has a built-in podcast directory:
www.apple.com/itunes

Libsyn
This podcast hosting service also offers subscribers a smartphone app:
www.libsyn.com

Podcast.com
Every podcaster should take a look at the 'ultimate podcast collection':
www.podcast.com

Podcast Advice
You'll find easy-to-read advice for podcasting beginners at:
www.podcastadvice.co.uk

Podcast Directory
This directory has links to podcasts from around the world:
www.podcastdirectory.com

Pod0matic
A podcast hosting service and directory:
www.pod0matic.com

The Podcast Guy
You'll discover advice for beginners from an experienced podcaster, including example podcasts, at:
www.thepodcastguy.com

Video Editing Software
This site provides details of the ten best free video editing software packages:
www.akascope.com/2011/07/15/free-video-editing-software

YouTube
Upload and share your own video podcasts for free at:
www.youtube.com

INDEX